Your Gift of Grace

Tom J.

Tom Janicik

Your Gift of Grace

To:

_____

From:

_____

Date:

_____

Message:

_____

_____

_____

_____

_____

Jeremiah 29:13 And you will seek Me and find Me, when you search for Me with all your heart.

Your Gift of Grace

Contents

Chapter I - Brighter Day

Chapter II - Recreated

Chapter III - Treasures in Heaven

Chapter IV – My Lighthouse

Dedication

For never giving up on me, I dedicate this book to my Creator. May Your Light shine bright upon those who will open their hearts to hear Your wondrous voice.

Acknowledgements

To my parents, Al and Eileen, who have been blessed with over 50 years of marriage. Thank you for instilling in me your values of loving and sacrificing for the sake of your children.

To my children, Elena and Tommy, you are my most precious gift. Thank you for providing me with your love, support, and talent.

To my editor, Mrs. Patricia Campbell, thank you for your inspiring feedback, insights, and commitment to detail.

Inspiration

Dear God,

These poems reflect my relationship with You, my Creator. Most of my life I have viewed religion as a social activity or routine with very little meaning or purpose. Not until my darkest hour of need, did You graciously connect directly to me (without even my request), letting me know that You truly do exist. I can still remember Your presence entering my body and soul during that flight from Houston to St. Louis back in June of 1998. You instantaneously brought an overwhelming sense of joy during the saddest part of my life, when I began to realize my marriage of almost 10 years was headed for inevitable divorce.

Since that time, You, Lord, and I have continued to grow closer each and every day. Thank you for helping me to uncover the buried gift with which you have blessed me. May it serve Your higher purpose rather than my own self-interests. May You use these words to touch the hearts of those who know You and especially those who don't know You yet, drawing them ever closer to Your Almighty presence.

My deepest desire is that after I leave this world, You will let me know that this book is something that brings You great joy. Until that time, I remain faithfully Yours.

Love,

Tom

My Reflections

The "My Reflections" space on the opposite page provides an opportunity for you after reading my poem and God's scripture to contemplate your own experiences and relationship with God. You might want to jot down some notes, draw a picture, or possibly create a poem of your own … whatever expression best suits you.

Consider reading one poem daily and capture your thoughts. After reading one, your reflections might begin with:

1) **Looking Upward** – Why are you thankful to God today?
2) **Searching Inward** – Through this message how is God strengthening you?
3) **Reaching Outward** – What simple acts of love or kindness could you share with someone today?

My prayer is that God will speak to you through this experience in some special way … as He has done so graciously to me.

Chapter I – Brighter Day

Brighter Day

In the wake of dawn
The sun shines bright
Upon my sleepy eyes
Wondering what trials this day will bring

Shall I choose the seemingly attractive
Yet darker abyss
Or steer towards the challenging
Yet brighter path to glory

Struggling between
My own self-interests
Versus submitting
To pure obedience

Today's choice
Is made from an eternal perspective
And the Holy Spirit fills
My heart and soul

I ask my Heavenly Father
To bless this day
So that I will honor and serve Him
Like His faithful son, Jesus Christ

As the sun sets
And its after glow fades away
The moon rises and shines
Softly on my face

I lie in a restful peace
Feeling His warm presence
Knowing His overwhelming love
Will never end

John 1:4-5 In Him was life, and the life was the light of men. And the light shines in the darkness, and the darkness did not comprehend it.

My Reflections

Use These Hands

Oh dear Lord
Use these hands
To serve
Your ways
Not mine

Use these hands
To touch
Their precious hearts
And heal their overwhelming
Anguish and pain

Use these hands
To help them feel
Your never-ending love
To know
That You are real

Use these hands
To bring them back
To the source
Of Your warmth
And comforting Light

Use these hands
To help bear their pain
Like Your only Son
Hands nailed to the cross
Who died for all our sins

Raising my hands to You in praise
Oh dear Heavenly Father
Use these hands
Use these hands
Please, use these hands

Psalm 134:1-3 A Song of Ascents. Behold, bless the LORD, All *you* servants of the LORD, Who by night stand in the house of the LORD! Lift up your hands *in* the sanctuary, And bless the LORD. The LORD who made heaven and earth Bless you from Zion!

My Reflections

The Healer

From the inner being
One cannot see
Blind without the Light
Lost in darkness
Trapped within self

The healing begins
As the Holy Spirit enters
A transfusion of power
Connects heart, body, and soul
And life is anew

Purpose,
Contentment,
And clarity abound
Inner peace is present
In the midst of life's storms

Destined to serve
Not self
Not things
Only the Master
Our Lord, Jesus Christ

Matthew 9:10-13 Now it happened, as Jesus sat at the table in the house, that behold, many tax collectors and sinners came and sat down with Him and His disciples. And when the Pharisees saw it, they said to His disciples, "Why does your Teacher eat with tax collectors and sinners?" When Jesus heard that, He said to them, "Those who are well have no need of a physician, but those who are sick. But go and learn what this means: 'I desire mercy and not sacrifice.' For I did not come to call the righteous, but sinners, to repentance."

My Reflections

_____

_____

_____

_____

_____

_____

_____

_____

_____

Sinking in Sorrow

Sadness floods my soul
Tears pour down
Like a river
Mourning and sorrow
Hold me down
Like a heavy weight
Around my neck
My head just above
The surface of restless waters

Water keeps rising
The load keeps pulling me down
My mouth will soon
Pass the water line
With my last breath
Just before going under
I beg you, Lord,
Please release this anchor
Before I drowned

Psalm 69:1-3 Save me, O God! For the waters have come up to my neck. I sink in deep mire, Where there is no standing; I have come into deep waters, Where the floods overflow me. I am weary with my crying; My throat is dry; My eyes fail while I wait for my God.

My Reflections

Handing It Over

Believing in God
Trusting in Him
Taking my anxiety
Handing it over to Him
Letting Him carry the load

Walking with Him
Holding His hand
Trusting His lead
Using His gifts
Serving His will

Restoring my spirit
Healing my heart
Calming my mind
Strengthening my will
Feeling His wondrous love

Matthew 11:28-30 Come to Me, all you who labor and are heavy laden, and I will give you rest. Take My yoke upon you and learn from Me, for I am gentle and lowly in heart, and you will find rest for your souls. For My yoke is easy and My burden is light."

My Reflections

_____

_____

_____

_____

_____

_____

_____

_____

_____

Whiter Than Snow

Dear God
You have given me the strength
To look inside myself
And see the darkness within

My pile of sins
Overfills the canyon of death
Overwhelming regret and remorse
Torment my soul

Tremendous guilt and shame
Possess my heart and mind
For not honoring You
All of these years

I beg You to show mercy
Upon my tarnished soul
To erase forever
This separation between us

Please, cleanse my spirit
Please, cleanse my heart
Please, cleanse my mind
Whiter than snow

Psalm 51:1-8 Have mercy upon me, O God, According to Your loving kindness; According to the multitude of Your tender mercies, Blot out my transgressions. Wash me thoroughly from my iniquity, And cleanse me from my sin. For I acknowledge my transgressions, And my sin is always before me. Against You, You only, have I sinned, And done this evil in Your sight— That You may be found just when You speak, And blameless when You judge. Behold, I was brought forth in iniquity, And in sin my mother conceived me. Behold, You desire truth in the inward parts, And in the hidden part You will make me to know wisdom. Purge me with hyssop, and I shall be clean; Wash me, and I shall be whiter than snow. Make me to hear joy and gladness, That the bones You have broken may rejoice.

My Reflections

Connection

Acknowledging
Your ever steadfast presence
My Creator
Looking inside myself
Seeing my sinful nature
And selfish driven desires

Accepting
Your gift of grace
Through Your only Son's
Ultimate sacrifice
Placing my life into His hands
Receiving His overwhelming love

Striving
To serve Your will
And not my own
Stumbling along the way
Asking forgiveness
For myself and for others

Growing
Closer to You
In a deeply intimate relationship
Through the powerful
Presence of Your
Holy Spirit

Yearning
To be with You now
And forever in heaven
But torn with the desire
To stay and to share
Your good news with others

Luke 11:33-36 "No one, when he has lit a lamp, puts it in a secret place or under a basket, but on a lampstand, that those who come in may see the light. The lamp of the body is the eye. Therefore, when your eye is good, your whole body also is full of light. But when your eye is bad, your body also is full of darkness. Therefore take heed that the light which is in you is not darkness. If then your whole body is full of light, having no part dark, the whole body will be full of light, as when the bright shining of a lamp gives you light."

My Reflections

Unity

Created
In Your image
Hearts connected as one
Unity
In mind, body, spirit and soul

Belief based on
Transparent truth
Impenetrable faith
By the power
Of Your Holy Spirit

Through Your eyes
Able to see
Self's natural attraction
To destructive darkness
Able to choose Your will

Intense passion
To serve obediently
Your purpose
Joyfully dwelling together as one
In Your overwhelming love

John 17:20-26 "I do not pray for these alone, but also for those who will believe in Me through their word; that they all may be one, as You, Father, are in Me, and I in You; that they also may be one in Us, that the world may believe that You sent Me. And the glory which You gave Me I have given them, that they may be one just as We are one: I in them, and You in Me; that they may be made perfect in one, and that the world may know that You have sent Me, and have loved them as You have loved Me. Father, I desire that they also whom You gave Me may be with Me where I am, that they may behold My glory which You have given Me; for You loved Me before the foundation of the world. O righteous Father! The world has not known You, but I have known You; and these have known that You sent Me. And I have declared to them Your name, and will declare it, that the love with which You loved Me may be in them, and I in them."

My Reflections

Hardened Heart

Years of pain and shame
Suppressed down deep
Love is present
But somehow disappears

Piercing of the heart
Relentlessly, over and over
One small blow at a time
Until the scars grew very hard and rigid

Life exists from a self-centered view
Concerned mostly with protecting self
Compassion for others and their needs
Has all but disappeared

Life is very lonely and unfulfilling
Driven to achieve
More for self
But never feeling good enough

Then Your glorious Grace
Infuses my heart
And touches my soul
Transformed forever

And so the healing begins
My heart growing softer day by day
Remembering like a child
Being more open, vulnerable and caring

Knowing that no matter what
You will protect me
My eternal parent
Forever in adoration of Your limitless mercy

Matthew 13:14-15 And in them the prophecy of Isaiah is fulfilled, which says: 'Hearing you will hear and shall not understand, And seeing you will see and not perceive; For the hearts of this people have grown dull. Their ears are hard of hearing, And their eyes they have closed, Lest they should see with their eyes and hear with their ears, Lest they should understand with their hearts and turn, So that I should heal them.'

My Reflections

Holy Spirit

Oh, heart open wide
Holy Spirit
Let Your light shine
Warm my heart
Touch my soul
Clear my thoughts
Draw me closer to Your presence
Fill me with Your never-ending love
Oh, mind be still
Show me the way of Your will
Give me the strength to obey Your desires
And the patience to wait on Your helping hand
Guide me through the raging storms of life
Shine Your beacon bright
So that I will choose to follow Your path
And not my own
In Jesus name, I pray
Amen

Jude 1:20-21 But you, beloved, building yourselves up on your most holy faith, praying in the Holy Spirit, keep yourselves in the love of God, looking for the mercy of our Lord Jesus Christ unto eternal life.

My Reflections

Through Your Eyes

Through Your eyes
Truth is transparent
Goodness shines
Bright in Your Light
And the darkness of evil
Is readily exposed

Through Your eyes
Love for others
Naturally exudes
From my compassionate heart
And an inner joy and peace
Soothes my soul

Through Your eyes
The mystery of life
Is unveiled
My reason for being
And life's purpose
Is quite clear

Through Your eyes
My will
Is to serve Yours
So that we are
Together as one
Now and forevermore

Matthew 6:22-23 "The lamp of the body is the eye. If therefore your eye is good, your whole body will be full of light. But if your eye is bad, your whole body will be full of darkness. If therefore the light that is in you is darkness, how great is that darkness!

My Reflections

Lost Then Found

The world spins around me
Everything moving so fast
Searching for direction
Lost between self
And the desires of others

Driven to succeed
Learning more
Controlling more
Striving for more
Obtaining more
But somehow the cup
Is always half empty

Who am I
Why am I here
What purpose does my life have
What is my destiny

Inevitably, trauma rocks my world
Turning things upside down
Completely vulnerable
And sinking fast
No chance for recovery
Overwhelmed by anguish and pain

Somehow, out of nowhere
Your merciful hand
Touches my broken soul
Shining down
Filling my emptiness
Breaking through my hardened heart

Realizing, that You truly do exist
Knowing, Your love will never end
Understanding, why I am here
Growing, closer to You
Sharing, You with others

Luke 15:3-7 So He spoke this parable to them, saying: "What man of you, having a hundred sheep, if he loses one of them, does not leave the ninety-nine in the wilderness, and go after the one which is lost until he finds it? And when he has found it, he lays it on his shoulders, rejoicing. And when he comes home, he calls together his friends and neighbors, saying to them, 'Rejoice with me, for I have found my sheep which was lost!' I say to you that likewise there will be more joy in heaven over one sinner who repents than over ninety-nine just persons who need no repentance.

My Reflections

Unspeakable Love

I see you up there
Hanging on the cross
In such overwhelming pain and anguish
You chose to sacrifice Yourself
For my selfish and sinful desires
Which have separated me
From Your presence

In Your final breath
I hear your last request
Asking God for my forgiveness
He honors Your request
Conditional on my choice
To accept You in faith

After accepting
Your gracious offer
I am recreated in Your image
Bringing forth a new life
Receiving Your
Unspeakable love
Overwhelming joy
Complete in our eternal unity

May my every breath
Every heartbeat
Every thought
Every act
Give praise to You
My Savior
My Lord
My Healer

Romans 5:1-5 Therefore, having been justified by faith, we have peace with God through our Lord Jesus Christ, through whom also we have access by faith into this grace in which we stand, and rejoice in hope of the glory of God. And not only that, but we also glory in tribulations, knowing that tribulation produces perseverance; and perseverance, character; and character, hope. Now hope does not disappoint, because the love of God has been poured out in our hearts by the Holy Spirit who was given to us.

My Reflections

Reflection

Looking at my reflection
In the calming pool of water
I can see myself
For who I really am

My buried flaws
Readily standout
From the brightness
Of Your Light

Seeing that through
Reliance on self
My flaws systemically
Spread within

Realizing that through
Reliance on You
My flaws are erased
By Your loving grace

Purified through
Your perfect sacrifice
Empowered with the presence
Of Your Holy Spirit

Psalm 139:23-24 Search me, O God, and know my heart; Try me, and know my anxieties; And see if there is any wicked way in me, And lead me in the way everlasting.

My Reflections

Faith

One God
One life
One choice
To believe
Or not
To believe

Eternal life
In warm
Comforting light
Or cold
Dismal darkness

Choose deep
Down within
Your spirits
Heart soul

Without connection
Your fate
Is sealed

Humbly submit
Serving God

Receive grace

James 2:14-18 What does it profit, my brethren, if someone says he has faith but does not have works? Can faith save him? If a brother or sister is naked and destitute of daily food, and one of you says to them, "Depart in peace, be warmed and filled," but you do not give them the things which are needed for the body, what does it profit? Thus also faith by itself, if it does not have works, is dead. But someone will say, "You have faith, and I have works." Show me your faith without your works, and I will show you my faith by my works.

My Reflections

The Antidote

Stricken by poison
From the forbidden fruit
The venom spreads systemically
Throughout the generations
Is there an antidote
Or is death certain
Numbness invades my body
And the end is ever present

Dear God
Forgive me
Save my soul
Through the cleansing power
Of Your sacrificial lamb
Jesus Christ
My Savior
My Lord

John 1:29-34 The next day John saw Jesus coming toward him, and said, "Behold! The Lamb of God who takes away the sin of the world! This is He of whom I said, 'After me comes a Man who is preferred before me, for He was before me.' "I did not know Him; but that He should be revealed to Israel, therefore I came baptizing with water." And John bore witness, saying, "I saw the Spirit descending from heaven like a dove, and He remained upon Him. I did not know Him, but He who sent me to baptize with water said to me, 'Upon whom you see the Spirit descending, and remaining on Him, this is He who baptizes with the Holy Spirit.' "And I have seen and testified that this is the Son of God."

My Reflections

Thanksgiving

Dear Lord
Thank you
For touching my heart and soul
Making me a new creation
Bringing me into Your Light
Wrapping me safely beneath Your wings

Please let me know Your desires
Help me grow closer to You
And understand Your ways
Please give me Your power and strength
So that I might walk each day and night
Under Your watchful eye

Please lead me to serve You
And resist the temptations
Of the evil darkness
By spreading Your everlasting joy
And glorious grace
Upon Your lost children

Psalm 63:6-8 When I remember You on my bed, I meditate on You in the night watches. Because You have been my help, Therefore in the shadow of Your wings I will rejoice. My soul follows close behind You; Your right hand upholds me.

My Reflections

Life's Race

Divergent paths
Relentless obstacles
Striving for success
Persevering to the end

Struggling for direction
Choosing Your way
Being set free
To do Your will not mine

Experiencing infinite joy
Throughout the pain and suffering
Of life's tremendous
Trials and tribulations

Fighting for victory
Over evil
Through the awesome strength
Of Your almighty power

Knowing You are working
Through me
Relying on You
To win the eternal prize

2 Timothy 4:6-8 For I am already being poured out as a drink offering, and the time of my departure is at hand. I have fought the good fight, I have finished the race, I have kept the faith. Finally, there is laid up for me the crown of righteousness, which the Lord, the righteous Judge, will give to me on that Day, and not to me only but also to all who have loved His appearing.

My Reflections

Always by My Side

Always by my side
No matter what
You are there

Like a loving father
Who knows what I need
Not what I want

Like a nurturing mother
Who consoles me
Whenever I am hurt

Like a big brother
Who would gladly
Lay down his life for mine

Like a little sister
Whose loyalty and kindness
Lasts forever

Like a faithful spouse
Whose unconditional love
Never ends

Like a best friend
In whom I can completely
Place my faith and trust

Thank you, Lord
For shining Your Light
And destroying the darkness

2 Timothy 4:16-18 At my first defense no one stood with me, but all forsook me. May it not be charged against them. But the Lord stood with me and strengthened me, so that the message might be preached fully through me, and that all the Gentiles might hear. And I was delivered out of the mouth of the lion. And the Lord will deliver me from every evil work and preserve me for His heavenly kingdom. To Him be glory forever and ever. Amen!

My Reflections

_____

_____

_____

_____

_____

_____

_____

_____

_____

The Garden of Life

Everything in a season
A season for everything
Life founded on roots
Deep below the surface
With death creating rebirth

Seedlings break through
In the spring
Being nurtured
By the warm sunlight
And cleansing rain

Mature growth
In the summer
Fully blossoming fruit
With exquisite beauty
And enticing aroma

Full harvest
In the fall
With dramatic change
And magnificently vibrant colors
Sensing life's end

Barren cold beauty
In the winter
With a pure white
Blanketing of snow
Slipping into peaceful sleep

Matthew 7:17-20 Even so, every good tree bears good fruit, but a bad tree bears bad fruit. A good tree cannot bear bad fruit, nor can a bad tree bear good fruit. Every tree that does not bear good fruit is cut down and thrown into the fire. Therefore by their fruits you will know them.

My Reflections

Sunrise

Night's cold dark dampness
Is driven off
By the new morning sunrise
Breaking through the distant horizon
Spreading those golden rays
Of comforting warmth
Burning through the majestic mist

Your almighty presence
Shines brightly
Throughout all of creation
May Your Light
Continue to heal the lost
Bringing them eternal hope
Through Your glorious gift of grace

John 3:16 For God so loved the world that He gave His only begotten Son, that whoever believes in Him should not perish but have everlasting life.

My Reflections

Chapter II – Recreated

Recreated

Born in Your image
Yet separated from Your presence
By choosing my will
Over Yours

Drifting further
And further apart
Drowning in a sea
Of selfish desires

Finally recognizing Your existence
And in faith
Choosing to submit
My will to Yours

Instantaneously
Recreated
Through the power
Of Your Holy Spirit

Openly admitting
My transgressions against You
Sensing deep remorse and sadness
From the distance between us

Amazed by Your gracious
Offer to wipe
The slate clean
And start over anew

Thoughts in my mind
Focus on Your will
Our hearts joined compassionately
Together forever as one

Galatians 5:22-26 But the fruit of the Spirit is love, joy, peace, longsuffering, kindness, goodness, faithfulness, gentleness, self-control. Against such there is no law. And those who are Christ's have crucified the flesh with its passions and desires. If we live in the Spirit, let us also walk in the Spirit. Let us not become conceited, provoking one another, envying one another.

My Reflections

_____

_____

_____

_____

_____

_____

_____

_____

_____

The Struggle Within

Dear Heavenly Father
My mind relentlessly
Draws me back to self's desires
Which hardens my heart
And pulls me further away
From Your warm presence

Please break these chains
Which hold me back
Free me from my selfishness
So that I will come
To know and serve
Your will and not my own

Draw me to Your presence
For without You
I have no purpose
Show me the way
Show me the truth
Show me the life

Use me as a beacon
To touch the hearts
Of Your lost children
So that they might know You
My glorious Creator
My ever loving and faithful Father
My gracious Redeemer

2 Timothy 2:8-13 Remember that Jesus Christ, of the seed of David, was raised from the dead according to my gospel, for which I suffer trouble as an evildoer, even to the point of chains; but the word of God is not chained. Therefore I endure all things for the sake of the elect, that they also may obtain the salvation which is in Christ Jesus with eternal glory. This is a faithful saying: For if we died with Him, We shall also live with Him. If we endure, We shall also reign with Him. If we deny Him, He also will deny us. If we are faithless, He remains faithful; He cannot deny Himself.

My Reflections

Contentment

Trusting in God
Selflessly serving Him
Expecting nothing in return
Receiving Your eternal reward

Philippians 4:10-13 But I rejoiced in the Lord greatly that now at last your care for me has flourished again; though you surely did care, but you lacked opportunity. Not that I speak in regard to need, for I have learned in whatever state I am, to be content: I know how to be abased, and I know how to abound. Everywhere and in all things I have learned both to be full and to be hungry, both to abound and to suffer need. I can do all things through Christ who strengthens me.

My Reflections

Strength in Weakness

It's amazing how
My greatest strength arises
During my weakest moments
How can this be

Maybe because You
Like to test me
To see if I will truly
Place my complete faith and trust in You

Tremendous power occurs
When I rely on You
An unshakable strength
That can be found no where else

Even during my most hopeless moments
Your warm and radiant light
Shines through to my heart and soul
As we walk together hand in hand

Psalm 18:16-19 He sent from above, He took me; He drew me out of many waters. He delivered me from my strong enemy, From those who hated me, For they were too strong for me. They confronted me in the day of my calamity, But the LORD was my support. He also brought me out into a broad place; He delivered me because He delighted in me.

My Reflections

Rejoice

Oh, dear God
Why did I deny You all of these years
Why did I chose to serve myself
Instead of You, my Creator
How could I be so foolish

Why did You give me my own free will
To believe and trust in You
Or deny Your existence
And sentence myself to eternal isolation
From Your overwhelming love

Why did You come down
And break through to my soul
In my darkest hour of need
When the losses were huge
But the gain was infinite

You are my eternal Father
Whose love runs so incredibly deep
You choose to save me
When I needed You most
Reuniting us forevermore

My debt to You can never be repaid
By Your grace I have been saved
I rejoice in You, my Father
And in Your Son's ultimate sacrifice
And in Your Holy Spirit's presence

Lead me to understand Your will
Throughout the rest of my life
So that I will honor and serve You
Show me Your way
And I will follow

Psalm 57:7-11 My heart is steadfast, O God, my heart is steadfast; I will sing and give praise. Awake, my glory! Awake, lute and harp! I will awaken the dawn. I will praise You, O Lord, among the peoples; I will sing to You among the nations. For Your mercy reaches unto the heavens, And Your truth unto the clouds. Be exalted, O God, above the heavens; Let Your glory be above all the earth.

My Reflections

Solemn Silence

Bathing in
Solemn silence
Your calming spirit
Soothes my soul

Knowing that
You are with me
Watching over me
Leading me toward the Light

My heart abounds in joy
Dwelling in Your presence
Sensing Your warm touch
Ever grateful for Your mercy

Rejoicing for the day
We will be reunited
Forever in eternity
With all of Your faithful children

Psalm 19:1-4 The heavens declare the glory of God; And the firmament shows His handiwork. Day unto day utters speech, And night unto night reveals knowledge. There is no speech nor language. Where their voice is not heard. Their line has gone out through all the earth, And their words to the end of the world.

My Reflections

Real Love

Love for a child is
Real love
Which comes from above

Father, You sacrificed
Your only son
For my sake

Always hoping that
I would humbly accept
Your gift of grace

Acknowledging my transgressions
I accept Your offer
Of redemption

Recreated by Your
Real love
Which comes from above

1 John 4:9-10 In this the love of God was manifested toward us, that God has sent His only begotten Son into the world, that we might live through Him. In this is love, not that we loved God, but that He loved us and sent His Son to be the propitiation for our sins.

My Reflections

Letting Go

Living life's delusion
Constantly attempting
To control everything
Unaware of Your ever presence

Struggling to succeed
On my own
All alone
Slave to self's desire

Then one day
You miraculously arrive
Like a lightning bolt
Breaking through these heavy chains

Freedom occurs
By serving Your will
And simply
Letting go

1 Corinthians 7:20-24 Let each one remain in the same calling in which he was called. Were you called while a slave? Do not be concerned about it; but if you can be made free, rather use it. For he who is called in the Lord while a slave is the Lord's freedman. Likewise he who is called while free is Christ's slave. You were bought at a price; do not become slaves of men. Brethren, let each one remain with God in that state in which he was called.

My Reflections

Invaluable Treasure

Our relationship
Is an invaluable treasure
Worthy of never ending praise

Your Holy nature
Draws me to revere You deeply
My strongest desire is to emulate Your love

By completely surrendering
My will to Yours
Peaceful waters calmly cleanse my soul

Let Your almighty power
Shine through me as a brightly lit beacon
Blessing all of Your beautiful children

1 Peter 1:13-16 Therefore gird up the loins of your mind, be sober, and rest your hope fully upon the grace that is to be brought to you at the revelation of Jesus Christ; as obedient children, not conforming yourselves to the former lusts, as in your ignorance; but as He who called you is holy, you also be holy in all your conduct, because it is written, "Be holy, for I am holy."

My Reflections

_____

_____

_____

_____

_____

_____

_____

_____

_____

You Are with Me

Looking upward through the billowy clouds
I can sense Your majestic face
Gently watching over me
Your reflection freely floating
Over the pools of calm water

I can hear Your voice
Calling out my name
Carefully guiding me to safe shelter
From the ominous storm of darkness
Mounting on the horizon

I can feel Your presence
Through the sun's rays
Shining down upon me
My spirit dances in the rising winds
As You graciously caress my soul

Exodus 33:17-23 So the LORD said to Moses, "I will also do this thing that you have spoken; for you have found grace in My sight, and I know you by name." And he said, "Please, show me Your glory." Then He said, "I will make all My goodness pass before you, and I will proclaim the name of the LORD before you. I will be gracious to whom I will be gracious, and I will have compassion on whom I will have compassion." But He said, "You cannot see My face; for no man shall see Me, and live." And the LORD said, "Here is a place by Me, and you shall stand on the rock. So it shall be, while My glory passes by, that I will put you in the cleft of the rock, and will cover you with My hand while I pass by. Then I will take away My hand, and you shall see My back; but My face shall not be seen."

My Reflections

Praise to You, Father

Praise to You, Father
May Your almighty power
Reign forevermore

Praise to You, Father
May our songs of adoration
Ascend towards Your heavens

Praise to You, Father
May Your glory and majesty
Be revered by all Your precious children

Praise to You, Father
May Your endless love
Keep our hearts pure

Praise to You, Father
May we honor and respect
Your perfect plan for our lives

Praise to You, Father
May we always treasure
Your Son's glorious gift of grace

Praise to You, Father
For feeding our weary souls
With Your Holy Spirit

Praise to You, Father
May we joyously
Exalt You forever

Psalm 150:1–6 Praise the LORD! Praise God in His sanctuary; Praise Him in His mighty firmament! Praise Him for His mighty acts; Praise Him according to His excellent greatness! Praise Him with the sound of the trumpet; Praise Him with the lute and harp! Praise Him with the timbrel and dance; Praise Him with stringed instruments and flutes! Praise Him with loud cymbals; Praise Him with clashing cymbals! Let everything that has breath praise the LORD. Praise the LORD!

My Reflections

Can You Feel the Rhythm

Can you feel the rhythm
When the morning bird
Sings songs of praise

Can you feel the rhythm
When the ocean's waves
Swell gently back and forth

Can you feel the rhythm
When the circling wind
Caresses the dancing leaves

Can you feel the rhythm
When the peaceful sun's beauty
Settles down for the evening

Can you feel the rhythm
When the full moon's bright shine
Inspires the cricket's melody

Can you feel the rhythm
When His presence
Dwells down deep in your soul

Psalm 149:1-5 Praise the LORD! Sing to the LORD a new song, And His praise in the assembly of saints. Let Israel rejoice in their Maker; Let the children of Zion be joyful in their King. Let them praise His name with the dance; Let them sing praises to Him with the timbrel and harp. For the LORD takes pleasure in His people; He will beautify the humble with salvation. Let the saints be joyful in glory; Let them sing aloud on their beds.

My Reflections

_____

_____

_____

_____

_____

_____

_____

_____

_____

Imagine

Imagine a supreme love
Which shines down from above
Filling your heart
With complete contentment

Imagine a mind
Which clearly knows
Good from evil
Instinctively choosing the righteous path to glory

Imagine a spirit
Who communes forever
With the Almighty Creator
Where time has no meaning

Imagine a world
Whose unified faith
Is witnessed by an impenetrable
Trust in God

Imagine a life
Where success is measured
By how one serves
The needs of others

Imagine celebrating a physical death
Which opens the door
To an eternal life
Free from the terminal disease of sin

Ephesians 3:14-19 For this reason I bow my knees to the Father of our Lord Jesus Christ, from whom the whole family in heaven and earth is named, that He would grant you, according to the riches of His glory, to be strengthened with might through His Spirit in the inner man, that Christ may dwell in your hearts through faith; that you, being rooted and grounded in love, may be able to comprehend with all the saints what is the width and length and depth and height— to know the love of Christ which passes knowledge; that you may be filled with all the fullness of God.

My Reflections

You Make Me Whole

You bring me strength
When I am weak

You calm my fears
When I lose control

You fill me with Your presence
When I am lonely

You erase my doubts
When I question my faith

You give me patience
When I am anxious

You cleanse my heart
When I am tempted by sin

You refresh my mind
When I'm drawn to self's desires

You feed my soul
When I am tired and hungry

You always forgive me
When I truly repent of my sins

You carefully guide me
When I am lost

You love me unconditionally
Even when I am not deserving

You make me whole
In heart, mind, body and soul

1 Thessalonians 5:23-24 Now may the God of peace Himself sanctify you completely; and may your whole spirit, soul, and body be preserved blameless at the coming of our Lord Jesus Christ. He who calls you is faithful, who also will do it.

My Reflections

My Secret Place

Stepping into the serenity
Of my secret place
Your overwhelming presence
Surrounds my weary soul
My eyes are closed in reverence
My ears carefully listen for Your voice
My mind rests at peace
My heart's desire is to be purified
My will freely submits to Yours

The palms of my hands
Rise up to You in humble gratitude
Praising You for Your
Never ending gift of grace
My spirit joyously basks
In the warm comforting glow
Of Your glorious Light
Which never ends

Matthew 6:1-6 "Take heed that you do not do your charitable deeds before men, to be seen by them. Otherwise you have no reward from your Father in heaven. Therefore, when you do a charitable deed, do not sound a trumpet before you as the hypocrites do in the synagogues and in the streets, that they may have glory from men. Assuredly, I say to you, they have their reward. But when you do a charitable deed, do not let your left hand know what your right hand is doing, that your charitable deed may be in secret; and your Father who sees in secret will Himself reward you openly. "And when you pray, you shall not be like the hypocrites. For they love to pray standing in the synagogues and on the corners of the streets, that they may be seen by men. Assuredly, I say to you, they have their reward. But you, when you pray, go into your room, and when you have shut your door, pray to your Father who is in the secret place; and your Father who sees in secret will reward you openly.

My Reflections

Always Faithful to the Cast

Sensing Your comforting presence
Serving Your will
Requesting Your help along the way
Always faithful to the cast

Accepting whatever You provide
Knowing that it is in my best interest
Relinquishing my doubts to You
Always faithful to the cast

Setting my sight on Your ways
Striving for the higher ground
Sharing Your good news with others
Always faithful to the cast

Anchoring my lifeline
To You
My Rock, my Savior, my Lord
Always faithful to the cast

Watching another day come to an end
Accepting your unconditional love
Being content in Your Spirit
Always faithful to the cast

Mark 1:16-18 And as He walked by the Sea of Galilee, He saw Simon and Andrew his brother casting a net into the sea; for they were fishermen. Then Jesus said to them, "Come after Me, and I will make you become fishers of men." And immediately they left their nets and followed Him.

My Reflections

Together

Dear Heavenly Father
May our relationship
Grow from below the surface
Where the hidden roots
Dig deeper and deeper
Intertwined in an ever binding love
Warmed by the goodness
Of Your sunshine
Fed by Your fertile Spirit
Refreshed by the quenching
Of Your cleansing rain
May our fragrant blossoms
Attract the wanderers
May our fruit
Feed their hunger
May our hearts
Sing together in harmony
And may our spirits
Dance together
Forever, as one

Colossians 3:12-15 Therefore, as the elect of God, holy and beloved, put on tender mercies, kindness, humility, meekness, longsuffering; bearing with one another, and forgiving one another, if anyone has a complaint against another; even as Christ forgave you, so you also must do. But above all these things put on love, which is the bond of perfection. And let the peace of God rule in your hearts, to which also you were called in one body; and be thankful.

My Reflections

Seduction

Like a moth
Drawn to the blinding light
Unable to resist
The seductive allure

Flying hypnotically
Round and round
Sensing the warmth
Driven to come closer

Finally, unable to stop
Plunging toward
The center of the light
Scorched by the torrid heat

Full of darkness

Matthew 18:7-9 Woe to the world because of offenses! For offenses must come, but woe to that man by whom the offense comes! If your hand or foot causes you to sin, cut it off and cast it from you. It is better for you to enter into life lame or maimed, rather than having two hands or two feet, to be cast into the everlasting fire. And if your eye causes you to sin, pluck it out and cast it from you. It is better for you to enter into life with one eye, rather than having two eyes, to be cast into hell fire.

My Reflections

Poisonous Pride

Poisonous pride
Truly the root
Of all evil
Self's deceptive desires
Fuel an inward
Pompous piety
Elevating one's ego
Only to look down
Upon others
Surrounded by the numbing darkness
Trapped in conceited contempt
Driven to increase knowledge
But lacking true wisdom
Constantly positioning self
For praise, honor and esteem
Only to receive
Shallow rewards and shame
Suffering from the terminal illness
Of a cold, hardened heart
Which can only be cured
By humbly submitting
To the one and only, Creator
Whose merciful grace
Sets you free

Proverbs 16:16-20 How much better to get wisdom than gold! And to get understanding is to be chosen rather than silver. The highway of the upright is to depart from evil; He who keeps his way preserves his soul. Pride goes before destruction, And a haughty spirit before a fall. Better to be of a humble spirit with the lowly, Than to divide the spoil with the proud. He who heeds the word wisely will find good, And whoever trusts in the LORD, happy is he.

My Reflections

Heaven on Earth

Oh dear Heavenly Father
How grateful I am
For Your gracious act
Of loving kindness

Saving my soul
Without even a request
Knowing when I was in need
Caring enough to shine down upon me

Your warmth radiates
Throughout my heart, body and soul
Comforting me
Throughout all of life's sorrows

Please keep Your covenant
With me forever
By giving me the strength
To rely upon You

Please give me the wisdom
To listen and understand Your ways
So that I will submit my will
To faithfully serve Yours

Without Your presence
I am lost
In cold bitter darkness, like
Hell on earth

With Your presence
I am found
In warm soothing light, like
Heaven on earth

Revelation 21:1-4 Now I saw a new heaven and a new earth, for the first heaven and the first earth had passed away. Also there was no more sea. Then I, John, saw the holy city, New Jerusalem, coming down out of heaven from God, prepared as a bride adorned for her husband. And I heard a loud voice from heaven saying, "Behold, the tabernacle of God is with men, and He will dwell with them, and they shall be His people. God Himself will be with them and be their God. And God will wipe away every tear from their eyes; there shall be no more death, nor sorrow, nor crying. There shall be no more pain, for the former things have passed away."

My Reflections

Save Another Soul

Dear Father in Heaven
Let Your wayward children
Experience the natural consequences
Of denying Your existence

Show them the darkness
That dwells within
Let them foresee their
Inevitable day of judgment

Please open their hearts
To hear Your voice
Please open their minds
To understand Your ways

Bring them truly to repent of their sins
Accepting Your gracious offer
Of complete forgiveness
Through the sacrifice of Your only son, Jesus Christ

Fill them with Your Holy Spirit
So they will experience
An intimate relationship with You
Full of the deepest form of love and contentment

Let them realize You control everything
Help them submit to You
So that You will
Save another soul

Mark 8:34-38 When He had called the people to Himself, with His disciples also, He said to them, "Whoever desires to come after Me, let him deny himself, and take up his cross, and follow Me. For whoever desires to save his life will lose it, but whoever loses his life for My sake and the gospel's will save it. For what will it profit a man if he gains the whole world, and loses his own soul? Or what will a man give in exchange for his soul? For whoever is ashamed of Me and My words in this adulterous and sinful generation, of him the Son of Man also will be ashamed when He comes in the glory of His Father with the holy angels."

My Reflections

_____

_____

_____

_____

_____

_____

_____

_____

_____

Lord's Blessing

May the Lord
Touch your heart
Filling your spirit with His presence

May He give you the love
That you have always longed for
But never have been able to find

May He lead your ways
As you grow together
In the deepest of all intimacy

May He always be by your side
Throughout life's peaks and valleys
Providing you with a calm inner strength

May His overwhelming love
Radiate to all who cross your path
Sharing His deepest desire

May He use your life
For His greater glory
And the benefit of others

May you celebrate together
Rejoicing over your eternal treasures
When you are forever reunited in heaven

Numbers 6:22-26 And the LORD spoke to Moses, saying: "Speak to Aaron and his sons, saying, 'This is the way you shall bless the children of Israel. Say to them: "The LORD bless you and keep you; the LORD make His face shine upon you, And be gracious to you; the LORD lift up His countenance upon you, and give you peace."'"

My Reflections

Recreated II

Everyday the darkness
Inside of me
Invades my heart, my mind, my soul
Leading me to harmful thoughts
And acts of disobedience

Your cleansing Light of truth
Allows me readily to see
This destructive force
Freely choosing
To serve Your will or my own

My deepest desire
Is being completely crucified to self
Recreated in Your perfect image
Faithfully serving You
My blessed Creator and eternal Father

Please give me the strength
To choose Your way
Everyday of my life
Touching the lives
Of those who seek Your love

I yearn for that day
When we are reunited
Forever free from this darkness
Which slithers inside of me
Always looking to strike in a moment of weakness

Galatians 2:17-21 But if, while we seek to be justified by Christ, we ourselves also are found sinners, is Christ therefore a minister of sin? Certainly not! For if I build again those things which I destroyed, I make myself a transgressor. For I through the law died to the law that I might live to God. I have been crucified with Christ; it is no longer I who live, but Christ lives in me; and the life which I now live in the flesh I live by faith in the Son of God, who loved me and gave Himself for me. I do not set aside the grace of God; for if righteousness comes through the law, then Christ died in vain."

My Reflections

Chapter III – Treasures In Heaven

Treasures in Heaven

As we draw closer
My heart's desire
Is to serve You faithfully
Building up eternal
Treasures in heaven

Please give me the strength
To call upon Your power
Receiving Your guidance
To serve Your will
And not my own

May our relationship
Grow stronger each day
Through faithful acts of kindness
Praising Your presence
Basking in Your joyful abundance

May we commune
Together as one
Shining brightly
Touching their hearts
Accepting Your limitless love

Matthew 6:19-21 "Do not lay up for yourselves treasures on earth, where moth and rust destroy and where thieves break in and steal; but lay up for yourselves treasures in heaven, where neither moth nor rust destroys and where thieves do not break in and steal. For where your treasure is, there your heart will be also.

My Reflections

_____

_____

_____

_____

_____

_____

_____

_____

_____

I Give Praise to You

Through the pain
That I must suffer
Not of my will
I give praise to You

Sensing Your presence
Gives me the strength
To live on
I give praise to You

Struggling to submit
My will
To Yours
I give praise to You

Wanting to hear
Your next step
For my life
I give praise to You

Asking Your Holy Spirit
To live in my soul
In order to serve Your will
I give praise to You

Letting my Sculptor
Mold me
In His ways
I give praise to You

Begging you to show
Your tender mercies
To all those who will listen
I give praise to You

Knowing that one day
We will be together as one
Forever free of pain and suffering
I give praise to You

Through all that is
Seen and unseen
My Heavenly Father
I give praise to You

2 Chronicles 5:13-14 … indeed it came to pass, when the trumpeters and singers were as one, to make one sound to be heard in praising and thanking the LORD, and when they lifted up their voice with the trumpets and cymbals and instruments of music, and praised the LORD, saying: "For He is good, For His mercy endures forever," that the house, the house of the LORD, was filled with a cloud, so that the priests could not continue ministering because of the cloud; for the glory of the LORD filled the house of God.

My Reflections

Please Show Me Your Way

Oh Lord
I love Thee
Most of all

Please show me
Please show me
Please show me Your way

Oh Lord
I love Thee
Most of all

Please show me
Please show me
Please show me Your way

Oh Lord
I love Thee
Most of all

Please show me
Please show me
Please show me Your way

Psalm 86:11-13 Teach me Your way, O LORD; I will walk in Your truth; Unite my heart to fear Your name. I will praise You, O Lord my God, with all my heart, And I will glorify Your name forevermore. For great is Your mercy toward me, And You have delivered my soul from the depths of Sheol.

My Reflections

As Iron Sharpens Iron

Brother in Christ
Remove the debris
Which torments our souls

Strike firm
With your sword
Refining us

As a sharp blade
Gleans brightly
In the light

So too shall
We shine
As iron sharpens iron

Proverbs 27:17 As iron sharpens iron, So a man sharpens the countenance of his friend.

My Reflections

Hosanna in the Highest

Heavenly Father
Almighty creator
Divine master
Everlasting
Ever righteous
Ever pure
Hosanna
Hosanna in the highest

Sacrificial Son
Of the Father
Savior of the world
All merciful comforter
Lord of Lords
My Prince of Peace
Hosanna
Hosanna in the highest

Holy Spirit
Ever present
Light of truth
Healer of the sick
Lover of the lost
Purifier of the soul
Hosanna
Hosanna in the highest

Everything I was
Everything I am
Everything I shall ever be
May it bring
Praise and glory
To Your name
Hosanna
Hosanna in the highest

Mark 11:9-10 Then those who went before and those who followed cried out, saying: "Hosanna! 'Blessed is He who comes in the name of the LORD!' Blessed is the kingdom of our father David that comes in the name of the Lord! Hosanna in the highest!"

My Reflections

Can You Hear His Voice

Can you hear His voice
Shining down upon you
When the sun's warm rays
Transcend your body and soul

Can you hear His voice
When the billowy clouds
Create beautiful images
Floating through the sky

Can you hear His voice
While the circling wind
Brings the rustling leaves
Alive into playful dance

Can you hear His voice
When the rhythmic waves
Caress the rugged shoreline
With peaceful songs of joy

Can you hear His voice
When you gaze upward
At the falling stars shining
Light across the dark horizon

Can you hear His voice
Echoing through the valley
Calling out your name
Asking if you will follow

Hebrews 4:7 … again He designates a certain day, saying in David, "Today," after such a long time, as it has been said: "Today, if you will hear His voice, Do not harden your hearts."

My Reflections

Everyday Idolatry

Everyday
Another idol
Raises its
Temptuous head

Constantly striving to
Permeate my will
Desiring to influence
My everyday choices

How foolish
Can I be
Not to see Your will
And faithfully follow

Help me to stop
Choosing my selfish desires
And keep my eyes
Fixed upon Yours

Let me not continue
To arouse Your anger
And suffer those certain consequences
Which torment my soul

Release my stubbornness
So that I will
Humbly submit and obey
Your almighty ways

Bring forth the power
Of Your Holy Spirit
To dwell within me
Giving You honor and praise

Purify my soul
Cleansing the darkness
That rests deep inside
The hidden crevices of my heart

May my pleasure
Come from striving to fulfill
Your passion and desire
For my life

Help me to give up
The ways of this world
In order to fulfill
Your glorious ways

Give me the strength
To place my trust in You
Taking each step in faith
Towards Your Light

Galatians 5:16-26 I say then: Walk in the Spirit, and you shall not fulfill the lust of the flesh. For the flesh lusts against the Spirit, and the Spirit against the flesh; and these are contrary to one another, so that you do not do the things that you wish. But if you are led by the Spirit, you are not under the law. Now the works of the flesh are evident, which are: adultery, fornication, uncleanness, lewdness, idolatry, sorcery, hatred, contentions, jealousies, outbursts of wrath, selfish ambitions, dissensions, heresies, envy, murders, drunkenness, revelries, and the like; of which I tell you beforehand, just as I also told you in time past, that those who practice such things will not inherit the kingdom of God. But the fruit of the Spirit is love, joy, peace, longsuffering, kindness, goodness, faithfulness, gentleness, self-control. Against such there is no law. And those who are Christ's have crucified the flesh with its passions and desires. If we live in the Spirit, let us also walk in the Spirit. Let us not become conceited, provoking one another, envying one another.

My Reflections

_____

_____

_____

_____

_____

_____

_____

_____

_____

Never Will I Forget

Never will I forget
My deadly sins
Which have caused
Our separation

Never will I forget
Your Father's act of love
Sending You down here
For my sake

Never will I forget
The indescribable anguish and pain
You suffered
On my behalf

Never will I forget
The nails that pierced
Your precious hands
Which healed my soul

Never will I forget
Your ever-forgiving heart
Which set me free
When I did not deserve to be

Never will I forget
Your limitless mercy
Your glorious grace
Your unbounded and amazing love

Psalm 119:93-96 I will never forget Your precepts, For by them You have given me life. I am Yours, save me; For I have sought Your precepts. The wicked wait for me to destroy me, But I will consider Your testimonies. I have seen the consummation of all perfection, But Your commandment is exceedingly broad.

My Reflections

Waiting on You

Waiting on You
Seems so hard to do
When I'm focused on me
And not upon You

Submitting my will
Obediently to serve Yours
Brings me to refreshing
Peaceful waters

Striving to move upstream
Against society's treacherous currents
Is truly an effort in futility
Without riding upon Your wings of Grace

Please give me the patience
To follow Your lead
Dwelling in the tranquil waters
Reflecting Your glorious face

Matthew 8:23-27 Now when He got into a boat, His disciples followed Him. And suddenly a great tempest arose on the sea, so that the boat was covered with the waves. But He was asleep. Then His disciples came to Him and awoke Him, saying, "Lord, save us! We are perishing!" But He said to them, "Why are you fearful, O you of little faith?" Then He arose and rebuked the winds and the sea, and there was a great calm. So the men marveled, saying, "Who can this be, that even the winds and the sea obey Him?"

My Reflections

Flicker of Faith

When the Light
Dims so low
Blown by the relentless winds
Near utter extinction

With just the smallest
Flicker of faith
He revives
Your soul

Gracefully
Breathing life
Into the fragile
Fire within

Spreading
His will throughout
Brightly burning
For all those choosing to believe

2 Timothy 1:5-7 ... when I call to remembrance the genuine faith that is in you, which dwelt first in your grandmother Lois and your mother Eunice, and I am persuaded is in you also. Therefore I remind you to stir up the gift of God which is in you through the laying on of my hands. For God has not given us a spirit of fear, but of power and of love and of a sound mind.

My Reflections

_____

_____

_____

_____

_____

_____

_____

_____

_____

Trapped

Trapped
In this earthly world
Able to see the seen
But not the unseen

Looking for a door
Which would reveal
The world beyond
Wondering if there really is one

Then one day You
Open the door
Through Your Son
Jesus Christ

Freely flowing faith
Knowing You are always
Ready to catch me
In Your outstretched hands

Requesting Your presence
To stay within my soul
Letting Your bright Light shine
For all to see

Ecclesiastes 9:12 For man also does not know his time: Like fish taken in a cruel net, Like birds caught in a snare, So the sons of men are snared in an evil time, When it falls suddenly upon them.

My Reflections

Breaking My Will

Breaking my will
Conforming to Yours

Destroying my pride
Shifting my eyes upon You

Strengthening my faith
Trusting in You

Purifying my mind
Thinking Your thoughts

Cleansing my spirit
Removing my sins

Softening my heart
Seeing their needs

Fueling my passion
Fulfilling their needs

Understanding Your direction
Obeying Your will

John 6:35-40 And Jesus said to them, "I am the bread of life. He who comes to Me shall never hunger, and he who believes in Me shall never thirst. But I said to you that you have seen Me and yet do not believe. All that the Father gives Me will come to Me, and the one who comes to Me I will by no means cast out. For I have come down from heaven, not to do My own will, but the will of Him who sent Me. This is the will of the Father who sent Me, that of all He has given Me I should lose nothing, but should raise it up at the last day. And this is the will of Him who sent Me, that everyone who sees the Son and believes in Him may have everlasting life; and I will raise him up at the last day."

My Reflections

_____

_____

_____

_____

_____

_____

_____

_____

_____

Please Draw Me Closer

Please draw me closer
To the source
Of Your warm
Comforting love

Please purify me
Through the eternal
Promise of Your
Sacrificial Son

Please fill me
With the almighty power
Of Your Holy Spirit
In order to serve Your will

Please show me Your path
Keep me from temptation
Shield me from evil
Staying within Your protective wings

Please strengthen my faith
Please deepen my trust
Please broaden my love
For You, my blessed Creator

Hebrews 10:19-25 Therefore, brethren, having boldness to enter the Holiest by the blood of Jesus, by a new and living way which He consecrated for us, through the veil, that is, His flesh, and having a High Priest over the house of God, let us draw near with a true heart in full assurance of faith, having our hearts sprinkled from an evil conscience and our bodies washed with pure water. Let us hold fast the confession of our hope without wavering, for He who promised is faithful. And let us consider one another in order to stir up love and good works, not forsaking the assembling of ourselves together, as is the manner of some, but exhorting one another, and so much the more as you see the Day approaching.

My Reflections

As Your Light Shines Down

As Your Light shines down
My entire body is enveloped
By Your radiant warmth
Bringing a comforting inner peace

As Your Light shines down
My mind is drawn to Yours
Freeing me from self's
Obsessions and desires

As Your Light shines down
My heart pounds in adoration
Ever thankful for being chosen
As one of Your faithful children

As Your Light shines down
Your Holy nature is revealed
My inherent flaws are readily exposed and erased
When I humbly request Your forgiveness

As Your Light shines down
My will submits to Yours
And our spirits are unified as one
Rejoicing in Your kingdom of glory

As Your Light shines down
Please use me as a beacon
That will touch the hearts
Of Your lost precious children

Luke 11:33-36 "No one, when he has lit a lamp, puts it in a secret place or under a basket, but on a lampstand, that those who come in may see the light. The lamp of the body is the eye. Therefore, when your eye is good, your whole body also is full of light. But when your eye is bad, your body also is full of darkness. Therefore take heed that the light which is in you is not darkness. If then your whole body is full of light, having no part dark, the whole body will be full of light, as when the bright shining of a lamp gives you light."

My Reflections

Ship Wrecked

Ship wrecked
Thrown overboard
Into the tumultuous seas
Where You are my lifesaver
Mercifully pulling me back

Lost
Without the Light
Which You provide
Shining a bright beacon
Leading me home to You

Saved
By Your Grace
Brought aboard Your ship
Capable of withstanding
The most torrential currents

Acts 27:39-44 When it was day, they did not recognize the land; but they observed a bay with a beach, onto which they planned to run the ship if possible. And they let go the anchors and left them in the sea, meanwhile loosing the rudder ropes; and they hoisted the mainsail to the wind and made for shore. But striking a place where two seas met, they ran the ship aground; and the prow stuck fast and remained immovable, but the stern was being broken up by the violence of the waves. And the soldiers' plan was to kill the prisoners, lest any of them should swim away and escape. But the centurion, wanting to save Paul, kept them from their purpose, and commanded that those who could swim should jump overboard first and get to land, and the rest, some on boards and some on parts of the ship. And so it was that they all escaped safely to land.

My Reflections

Light Your Fire

Light Your fire
Deep within my soul
Reviving those faint embers
Making them glow brightly
Breathing in life anew

Light Your fire
Within my heart
Stroking Your roaring
Eternal flames of love
Spreading Your radiant joy

Light Your fire
Within my mind
Seeing life clearly
Through Your eyes
Longing to fulfill Your will

Light Your fire
Fueling within me
Your intense passion
Spreading Your Light
Throughout this deceptive darkness

Light Your fire
Within Your inner circle
Exposing sin as sin
Recreating life by
Turning darkness into Light

Psalm 80:16-19 It is burned with fire, it is cut down; They perish at the rebuke of Your countenance. Let Your hand be upon the man of Your right hand, Upon the son of man whom You made strong for Yourself. Then we will not turn back from You; Revive us, and we will call upon Your name. Restore us, O LORD God of hosts; Cause Your face to shine, And we shall be saved!

My Reflections

Let Your Love Rain

Let Your love rain
Down on me
Cleansing
The eyes of my heart

Let Your love rain
Down on me
Purifying
The thoughts in my mind

Let Your love rain
Down on me
Renewing
My will to serve You

Let Your love rain
Down on me
Recreating
My soul in Your image

Let Your love rain
Down on me
Spreading
Your almighty reign

Isaiah 45:8 "Rain down, you heavens, from above, And let the skies pour down righteousness; Let the earth open, let them bring forth salvation, And let righteousness spring up together. I, the LORD, have created it.

My Reflections

Seeds of Love

May the gifts
You have blessed me with
Bring bountiful harvests
Of fruit which honors You

May You graft me
Into Your fertile vine
Uniting us together
Growing through Your Holy Spirit

May our blossoms
Magnificently bloom for all
To smell and taste
The sweetest of Your nectar

May You sow Your
Seeds of love
Ever expanding Your
Eternal tree of life

John 15:5-8 I am the vine, you are the branches. He who abides in Me, and I in him, bears much fruit; for without Me you can do nothing. If anyone does not abide in Me, he is cast out as a branch and is withered; and they gather them and throw them into the fire, and they are burned. If you abide in Me, and My words abide in you, you will ask what you desire, and it shall be done for you. By this My Father is glorified, that you bear much fruit; so you will be My disciples.

My Reflections

Bring Your Calmness

Bring Your calmness
To my heart and mind
Through Your ultimate sacrifice
Your grace and mercy sets me free

Bring Your calmness
To my soul
Through Your glorious presence
Your peace radiates within me

Bring Your calmness
To my will
Through my humble submission
Your plan is revealed

Bring Your calmness
To my faith
Through completely trusting in You
Your dreams are fulfilled

Psalm 46:10 Be still, and know that I am God; I will be exalted among the nations, I will be exalted in the earth!

My Reflections

Can You

Can You
Hear His voice
Calling out your name
Patiently asking you
To come back home

Can You
Feel His presence
Surrounding You
Always ready to catch you
When you fall

Can You
See His golden path
Laid down before you
Faithfully leading you
To everlasting glory

Can You
Smell the pleasing aroma
Circling upward to the heavens
Honoring His unconditional sacrifice
Which was fulfilled just for you

Can You
Taste the sweetest of all nectars
Fully blossoming
Through His everlasting love
Producing His eternal fruit

John 12:44-46 Then Jesus cried out and said, "He who believes in Me, believes not in Me but in Him who sent Me. And he who sees Me sees Him who sent Me. I have come as a light into the world, that whoever believes in Me should not abide in darkness.

My Reflections

Fixing My Eyes

Fixing my eyes
Upon the darkness
I am unsure of
Where I am going

Fixing my eyes
Upon Your cross
Your path burns brightly
Through the darkness

Fixing my eyes
Upon Your cross
My will submits joyfully
To serve Yours

Fixing my eyes
Upon Your cross
Your redemptive grace
Refreshes my spirit

Fixing my eyes
Upon Your cross
Your thoughts
Transform into mine

Fixing my eyes
Upon Your cross
Your overwhelming love
Overflows my empty heart

Fixing my eyes
Upon Your cross
Your fruit is bore
Through me

Fixing my eyes
Upon Your cross
Your eternal promise
Is fulfilled

Fixing my eyes
Upon Your cross
Your unlimited mercy and forgiveness
Transcends my soul

2 Corinthians 4:16-18 Therefore we do not lose heart. Even though our outward man is perishing, yet the inward man is being renewed day by day. For our light affliction, which is but for a moment, is working for us a far more exceeding and eternal weight of glory, while we do not look at the things which are seen, but at the things which are not seen. For the things which are seen are temporary, but the things which are not seen are eternal.

My Reflections

Free from Sin

Pure and righteous warrior
How I long for that day
That day of Your return
When You set me free
Free from sin

This sin down deep within
Breeding upon itself
Spreading like cancer
Searching to destroy
Whatever it might touch

King of Zion
Please come down
Cleanse me from this evil
Purify me through
Your perfect sacrifice

Blessed be that day
When Your kingdom is restored
And Your faithful sheep are delivered
Free from sin
This sin, which binds us

Romans 6:19-23 I speak in human terms because of the weakness of your flesh. For just as you presented your members as slaves of uncleanness, and of lawlessness leading to more lawlessness, so now present your members as slaves of righteousness for holiness. For when you were slaves of sin, you were free in regard to righteousness. What fruit did you have then in the things of which you are now ashamed? For the end of those things is death. But now having been set free from sin, and having become slaves of God, you have your fruit to holiness, and the end, everlasting life. For the wages of sin is death, but the gift of God is eternal life in Christ Jesus our Lord.

My Reflections

Your Cross

Your cross
Burns brightly
Through the hazy fog
Blazing truth

Your grace
Shines down
Through the warm sunlight
Radiating joy

Your mercy
Abounds limitlessly
Through the calming wind
Providing freedom

Your compassion
Runs deep
Through the canyon walls
Erasing those painful scars

Your love
Flows abundantly
Through the roaring river
Spreading eternal contentment

Philippians 3:17-21 Brethren, join in following my example, and note those who so walk, as you have us for a pattern. For many walk, of whom I have told you often, and now tell you even weeping, that they are the enemies of the cross of Christ: whose end is destruction, whose god is their belly, and whose glory is in their shame—who set their mind on earthly things. For our citizenship is in heaven, from which we also eagerly wait for the Savior, the Lord Jesus Christ, who will transform our lowly body that it may be conformed to His glorious body, according to the working by which He is able even to subdue all things to Himself.

My Reflections

For Such a Time As This

The stakes are too high
The future reaps utter despair
Turning to You for hope
Searching for guidance

Overwhelming fear of failure
Melts away with Your blazing Light
Gently handing it over to You
Letting You carry this unbearable load

Your overwhelming strength
Devours my weaknesses
Infusing an unbreakable confidence
By simply relying upon You

Whenever You call
Help me to hear
Your voice and
Follow Your lead

Ready to serve faithfully
Ready to act promptly
Ready to obey Your will
For such a time as this

Esther 4:12-15 So they told Mordecai Esther's words. Then Mordecai told them to answer Esther: "Do not think in your heart that you will escape in the king's palace any more than all the other Jews. For if you remain completely silent at this time, relief and deliverance will arise for the Jews from another place, but you and your father's house will perish. Yet who knows whether you have come to the kingdom for such a time as this?"

My Reflections

Chapter IV – My Lighthouse

My Lighthouse

Through the darkness
Your guiding Light
Gives me hope
Restoring my faith

Through the pounding surf
Your shining Light
Warms my heart
Renewing my mind

Through the howling wind
Your flickering Light
Calms my spirit
Soothing my soul

Through the treacherous waters
Your radiant Light
Helps me place my trust in You
Submitting to Your will

You alone are
My Lighthouse
May You use me
As a beacon of Your Light

John 12:35-36 Then Jesus said to them, "A little while longer the light is with you. Walk while you have the light, lest darkness overtake you; he who walks in darkness does not know where he is going. While you have the light, believe in the light, that you may become sons of light." These things Jesus spoke, and departed, and was hidden from them.

My Reflections

Searching To Serve

Searching to serve
Your glorious will
Striving to submit
Relinquishing control

Relying on you
For strength
For direction
For help

Acknowledging You for
Your unconditional love
Your limitless mercy and grace
Your passionate relentless pursuit

Ephesians 6:5-8 Bondservants, be obedient to those who are your masters according to the flesh, with fear and trembling, in sincerity of heart, as to Christ; not with eyeservice, as men-pleasers, but as bondservants of Christ, doing the will of God from the heart, with good will doing service, as to the Lord, and not to men, knowing that whatever good anyone does, he will receive the same from the Lord, whether he is a slave or free.

My Reflections

_____

_____

_____

_____

_____

_____

_____

_____

_____

_____

Purify My Heart

Your generous gift
Freedom of choice
Provides the greatest blessing
And the greatest curse
Ever given to mankind

Naturally driven
By self's desire
Separates us
Creating this cold lonely
Distance between us

Drifting far away
In this sea of darkness
Building thicker and thicker
Walls of isolation
Too blind even to see

Like a lost child
Fallen from his father's grace
I freely and repeatedly
Choose to disobey You
Driving us further and further apart

Missing this truest of all love
Searching so desperately
Craving throughout my entire life
Knowing something is missing
But unable to find it

Only through the realization
That I truly do need You
Can I allow Your presence to
Purify my heart
And restore our eternal relationship

If I would have only known
How deeply passionate Your desire is
For being reunited
What measures You will take
The lengths that You will go

Just as a father patiently
Waits on the front porch
Shining a bright Light
To help lead
His child back home

So You too
Shall wait for me
Always hoping
Always reaching out
Helping me return to You

Psalm 51:10-12 Create in me a clean heart, O God, And renew a steadfast spirit within me. Do not cast me away from Your presence, And do not take Your Holy Spirit from me. Restore to me the joy of Your salvation, And uphold me by Your generous Spirit.

My Reflections

Freedom from Fear

Only the wise
Reverently respect Him
Fearful of His
Almighty power
Humbly submitting
Honoring His will

Aligned with Him
Tremendous strength
Overflows from within
Instilling an unbreakable confidence
Erasing any doubts with
Freedom from fear

Isaiah 41:10 Fear not, for I am with you; Be not dismayed, for I am your God. I will strengthen you, Yes, I will help you, I will uphold you with My righteous right hand.'

My Reflections

I Love You, Lord

I Love You, Lord
My almighty Creator
My powerful Redeemer
My eternal Father

I Love You, Lord
My life's Foundation
My sole reason for existence
My spirit's one true desire

I Love You, Lord
My great Protector
My patient Mentor
My forever faithful Friend

I Love You, Lord
My generous Provider
My compassionate Nurturer
My miraculous Healer

I Love You, Lord
My covenant Keeper
My merciful Master
My passionate Pursuer

I Love You, Lord
My gracious Warrior
My divine Deliverer
My inevitable righteous Judge

I Love You, Lord
My Light through darkness
My ever-present Companion
My unlimited source of amazing joy

Psalm 18:1-3 I will love You, O LORD, my strength. The LORD is my rock and my fortress and my deliverer; My God, my strength, in whom I will trust; My shield and the horn of my salvation, my stronghold. I will call upon the LORD, who is worthy to be praised; So shall I be saved from my enemies.

My Reflections

Sanctify My Soul

Sanctify my soul
Saving me with Your grace
Connecting me to Your glory
Infusing me with Your heavenly joy

Sanctify my soul
Through Your blazing fire
Removing my impurities
Spreading Your passion for truth

Sanctify my soul
Through Your cleansing waters
Flowing freely with Your current
Carving out Your will

Sanctify my soul
Through Your perfect justice
Refining my flawed character
To reflect Yours

1 Thessalonians 5:23-24 Now may the God of peace Himself sanctify you completely; and may your whole spirit, soul, and body be preserved blameless at the coming of our Lord Jesus Christ. He who calls you is faithful, who also will do it.

My Reflections

Your Greatest Blessing

Through the pain
You draw me closer
Forcing me finally to surrender
Relinquishing my will for Yours
Placing my weary feet
Upon Your golden path

Through the pain
You gently care for my wounds
Striking though
My hardened heart
Healing my broken spirit
Nurturing my distant soul

Through the pain
You provide tremendous joy
When I turn to You
For help and direction
Relying on You
For protection and comfort

Through the pain
Life's true purpose
Becomes very clear
Freedom from self's
Destructive dark desires
Opens the door
To spending eternity with You

Through the pain
You carefully refine my character
Carved by Your meticulous hand
Etched with Your Holy imprint
Providing to me
Your greatest blessing

Ephesians 1:3-10 Blessed be the God and Father of our Lord Jesus Christ, who has blessed us with every spiritual blessing in the heavenly places in Christ, just as He chose us in Him before the foundation of the world, that we should be holy and without blame before Him in love, having predestined us to adoption as sons by Jesus Christ to Himself, according to the good pleasure of His will, to the praise of the glory of His grace, by which He has made us accepted in the Beloved. In Him we have redemption through His blood, the forgiveness of sins, according to the riches of His grace which He made to abound toward us in all wisdom and prudence, having made known to us the mystery of His will, according to His good pleasure which He purposed in Himself, that in the dispensation of the fullness of the times He might gather together in one all things in Christ, both which are in heaven and which are on earth — in Him.

My Reflections

Love Is And Love Is Not

Love is concerned for the welfare of others
Not of one's self-interest

Love serves with pleasure
Not expecting anything in return

Love listens attentively to others
Not being self-absorbed

Love freely forgives others
Not building up walls around a hardened
heart

Love gratefully acknowledges the smallest
act of kindness
Not taking it for granted

Love shares openly and honestly
Not with a closed, cold, distant heart

Love treasures deep understanding,
purpose and meaning
Not superficial appearances or beliefs

Love patiently waits
Not becoming intolerant or angry

Love gives whatever is necessary
Not spitefully holding back

Love demonstrates support for others
Not giving up on them

Love shows compassion for other's pain
Not cruel inconsideration

Love trusts others at their word
Not silently questioning hidden motives

Love celebrates each moment of life
Not being pre-occupied with the past or
the future

Love is true to commitments
Not giving into misleading feelings

Love is fueled with passion
Not uncaring indifference

Love is pure and genuine
Not manipulating or contrived

Love freely expresses true feelings
Not being repressed by fear

Love is unity with God
Not being controlled by self's desire

Love is blissful heavenly peace
Not a tortuous internal power struggle
from hell

1 Corinthians 13:4-8 Love suffers long and is kind; love does not envy; love does not parade itself, is not puffed up; does not behave rudely, does not seek its own, is not provoked, thinks no evil; does not rejoice in iniquity, but rejoices in the truth; bears all things, believes all things, hopes all things, endures all things. Love never fails …

My Reflections

Simple Pleasures

Simple pleasures
Bring such joy

Awakening from the harmony
Of the morning birds' melody

Smelling the fragrant roses
Climbing up the archway

Tasting the sweet golden honey
Created from the busy bees' toil

Watching the majestic clouds
Drifting effortlessly across the horizon

Being gently caressed
By the sun's warm embrace

Simple pleasures
Help me praise You

Psalm 16:11 You will show me the path of life; In Your presence is fullness of joy; At Your right hand are pleasures forevermore.

My Reflections

Set Me Free

Set me free
From this dreary cloud
That envelops me

Bringing my sprit
Down into the dismal depths
Of lonely despair

Break through
With Your Light
Piercing through this foggy haze

Refresh my soul
With Your spirit
Restoring my faith

Renew my mind
With Your ways
Transforming my will to Yours

Restore my battered heart
With Your unbounded love
Healing my gaping wounds

Psalm 142:5-7 I cried out to You, O LORD: I said, "You are my refuge, My portion in the land of the living. Attend to my cry, For I am brought very low; Deliver me from my persecutors, For they are stronger than I. Bring my soul out of prison, That I may praise Your name; The righteous shall surround me, For You shall deal bountifully with me."

My Reflections

Look Inside My Heart

Look inside my heart
Reveal the hidden darkness
Buried deep within
Allowing me truly to repent of my sins

Look inside my heart
Place my trust in you
Releasing the worries of this world
Placing my faith into Your hands

Look inside my heart
Crucify my desires
Honoring Your glorious gift of grace
Serving those in need

Look inside my heart
Bless me with prosperity
Refining my character with humility
Giving all credit to You

2 Chronicles 16:9 For the eyes of the LORD run to and fro throughout the whole earth, to show Himself strong on behalf of those whose heart is loyal to Him …

My Reflections

Please Take Me to Higher Ground

Please take me to higher ground
Remove me from the worries of this world
Draw me closer to Your presence
Fill me with Your never-ending love

Please take me to higher ground
Only You know what I truly need
Place my complete trust in You
Let Your peace reign within me

Please take me to higher ground
Shield me from the hidden traps
That surrounds me from all directions
Lead me to Your righteous path of glory

Please take me to higher ground
Calm my inner soul
Open my heart to Your words of truth
Compel me to fulfill Your will

Please take me to higher ground
Until that day
When we are reunited in heaven
Forever free of this pain and suffering

Psalm 61:1-4 Hear my cry, O God; Attend to my prayer. From the end of the earth I will cry to You, When my heart is overwhelmed; Lead me to the rock that is higher than I. For You have been a shelter for me, A strong tower from the enemy. I will abide in Your tabernacle forever; I will trust in the shelter of Your wings.

My Reflections

Open My Eyes

Open my eyes
To see their needs
Surrounding me
Like fallen leaves
Circling in the wind

Connect my heart
To feel their pain
Bringing Your warm compassion
Like the golden sunshine
Touching the harvest grain

Transform my will
To help them passionately
Serving with acts of kindness
Like loving parents
Caring for their children

Bring Your joy
To fill my spirit
Searching to help another
Like Your Son
Sacrificing for Your greater glory

Galatians 5:22-26 But the fruit of the Spirit is love, joy, peace, longsuffering, kindness, goodness, faithfulness, gentleness, self-control. Against such there is no law. And those who are Christ's have crucified the flesh with its passions and desires. If we live in the Spirit, let us also walk in the Spirit. Let us not become conceited, provoking one another, envying one another.

My Reflections

The Miracle in Me

Father
You amaze me
Knowing
Just when I needed You
Just when I would listen
Just when my world was shattering apart

Father
You amaze me
Choosing
To fill me
With Your presence
Walking with me
Showing me the way

Father
You amaze me
Sacrificing
Your Son
Just for my sins
Loving me more
Than life itself

Father
You amaze me
Thank You for Your mercy
Thank You for Your persistence
Thank You for Your grace
Thank You for creating
The miracle in me

Mark 9:39-41 But Jesus said, "Do not forbid him, for no one who works a miracle in My name can soon afterward speak evil of Me. For he who is not against us is on our side. For whoever gives you a cup of water to drink in My name, because you belong to Christ, assuredly, I say to you, he will by no means lose his reward.

My Reflections

Open Their Eyes

Open their eyes
To look within themselves
And see the deceptive sin
Which separates them from You

Open their hearts
To receive Your healing touch
And accept Your free gift of grace
Which breaks through their hidden bondage

Open their minds
To understand Your absolute truths
And believe in their compassionate Creator
Who longs to bring them back home

Open their will
To submit humbly to You
And to give praise to their glorious Redeemer
Who willingly paid the ultimate sacrifice

Open their spirit
To sense Your wondrous plans
And bring them to fulfillment
Through the power of Your Holy Spirit

Acts 26:12-18 "While thus occupied, as I journeyed to Damascus with authority and commission from the chief priests, at midday, O king, along the road I saw a light from heaven, brighter than the sun, shining around me and those who journeyed with me. And when we all had fallen to the ground, I heard a voice speaking to me and saying in the Hebrew language, 'Saul, Saul, why are you persecuting Me? It is hard for you to kick against the goads.' So I said, 'Who are You, Lord?' And He said, 'I am Jesus, whom you are persecuting. But rise and stand on your feet; for I have appeared to you for this purpose, to make you a minister and a witness both of the things which you have seen and of the things which I will yet reveal to you. I will deliver you from the Jewish people, as well as from the Gentiles, to whom I now send you, to open their eyes, in order to turn them from darkness to light, and from the power of Satan to God, that they may receive forgiveness of sins and an inheritance among those who are sanctified by faith in Me.'

My Reflections

Looking Up the Mountain

Looking up the mountain
You dwell upon its pinnacle
Watching down upon me
Leading me with Your gentle touch

Looking up the mountain
An empty golden chair
Covered in comforting red velour
Remains open for Your chosen one

Looking up the mountain
My children joyfully play
Basking in Your radiance
Warmed by the presence of Your Light

Looking up the mountain
Believers give constant praise
To their glorious Creator and Redeemer
Rejoicing in Your amazing gift of grace

Looking up the mountain
I fervently pray for those
Who are not present
Pleading with You to please save another

Revelation 21:10-14 And he carried me away in the Spirit to a great and high mountain, and showed me the great city, the holy Jerusalem, descending out of heaven from God, having the glory of God. Her light was like a most precious stone, like a jasper stone, clear as crystal. Also she had a great and high wall with twelve gates, and twelve angels at the gates, and names written on them, which are the names of the twelve tribes of the children of Israel: three gates on the east, three gates on the north, three gates on the south, and three gates on the west. Now the wall of the city had twelve foundations, and on them were the names of the twelve apostles of the Lamb.

My Reflections

_____

_____

_____

_____

_____

_____

_____

_____

Created in Your Image

Created in Your image
Given freedom of choice
To honor, respect and love You
Or live in isolation from You

Separated from You
By this divisive sin
Which flows rapidly through me
Like an insidious cancer

Recreated by You
Through mere acceptance
Of Your unmerited
Act of grace

Simply believing in faith
Your Son, Jesus Christ
Died for my sins
Opens Your door to eternal life

Ephesians 2:4-10 But God, who is rich in mercy, because of His great love with which He loved us, even when we were dead in trespasses, made us alive together with Christ (by grace you have been saved), and raised us up together, and made us sit together in the heavenly places in Christ Jesus, that in the ages to come He might show the exceeding riches of His grace in His kindness toward us in Christ Jesus. For by grace you have been saved through faith, and that not of yourselves; it is the gift of God, not of works, lest anyone should boast. For we are His workmanship, created in Christ Jesus for good works, which God prepared beforehand that we should walk in them.

My Reflections

Give Me Strength

Give me strength
When I am weak
Uncertain of Your will
Leaning towards my own

Clear my mind
Open my heart
To hear your voice
Deep down within my soul

Let Your ways
Flow through me
Free as the eagle
Soars over the canyon walls

Let Your love
Touch those around me
Showing Your awesome presence
Knowing that You are my God

Philippians 4:12-13 I know how to be abased, and I know how to abound. Everywhere and in all things I have learned both to be full and to be hungry, both to abound and to suffer need. I can do all things through Christ who strengthens me.

My Reflections

Forgive Me, Lord

Forgive me, Lord
Forgetting Your presence
When You are always there

Forgive me, Lord
For not listening
To Your voice

Forgive me, Lord
For disobeying Your will
Choosing my own instead

Forgive me, Lord
For falling short
Of Your blessed plan

Forgive me, Lord
For not sharing
Your good news

Forgive me, Lord
Please purify my soul
With Your tender mercies

Forgive me, Lord
So that I might be
Your faithful servant

Forgive me, Lord
My Almighty Redeemer
Sacred Keeper of Your New Covenant

Jeremiah 31:31-34 "Behold, the days are coming, says the LORD, when I will make a new covenant with the house of Israel and with the house of Judah— not according to the covenant that I made with their fathers in the day that I took them by the hand to lead them out of the land of Egypt, My covenant which they broke, though I was a husband to them, says the LORD. But this is the covenant that I will make with the house of Israel after those days, says the LORD: I will put My law in their minds, and write it on their hearts; and I will be their God, and they shall be My people. No more shall every man teach his neighbor, and every man his brother, saying, 'Know the LORD,' for they all shall know Me, from the least of them to the greatest of them, says the LORD. For I will forgive their iniquity, and their sin I will remember no more."

My Reflections

Living Water

Refreshing stream flowing
Through the gateway
Of Your paradise

Watching the crystal clear
Calm cleansing current
Calling out my name

Touching the surface
With my toe
Sensing Your presence

Walking into my ankles
Your healing power
Flows throughout my body

Wading into my knees
My spirit dances in delight
Along with the unblemished fish

Plunging into the deep waters
My entire being is purified
Rejoicing in our permanent reunion

Observing along the shoreline
Your eternal trees of life
Bearing an abundance of fruit

By Your mercy and grace
Life becomes everlasting
Through Your living water

John 7:37-38 On the last day, that great day of the feast, Jesus stood and cried out, saying, "If anyone thirsts, let him come to Me and drink. He who believes in Me, as the Scripture has said, out of his heart will flow rivers of living water."

My Reflections

Thank You, God

Thank You, God
For creating me
In Your sacred image

Thank You, God
For sacrificing Your only Son
To pay for my mistakes

Thank You, God
For not giving up on me
Even when I had lost faith in You

Thank You, God
For life's pain
Which draws me ever closer to
You

Thank You, God
For being my God
In whom I place my trust

Thank You, God
For giving me everything I need
Not everything I want

Thank You, God
For my family and friends
May You bless them always

Thank You, God
For offering me
Eternal life with You

Thank You, God
For Your never-ending
Passionate love

John 11:40-44 Jesus said to her, "Did I not say to you that if you would believe you would see the glory of God?" Then they took away the stone from the place where the dead man was lying. And Jesus lifted up His eyes and said, "Father, I thank You that You have heard Me. And I know that You always hear Me, but because of the people who are standing by I said this, that they may believe that You sent Me." Now when He had said these things, He cried with a loud voice, "Lazarus, come forth!" And he who had died came out bound hand and foot with graveclothes, and his face was wrapped with a cloth. Jesus said to them, "Loose him, and let him go."

My Reflections

The Love That Endures

The love that endures
Bears an eternal flame
Impossible to extinguish

The love that endures
Sacrifices oneself
For the sake of the other

The love that endures
Forgives
The gravest of mistakes

The love that endures
Shares with an open heart
Even when overwhelmed by fear

The love that endures
Reflects deep burning passion
Caring more for the other than one's self

The love that endures
Places complete trust in God
Accepting whatever He provides

Psalm 136:26 Oh, give thanks to the God of heaven! For His mercy endures forever.

My Reflections

_____

_____

_____

_____

_____

_____

_____

_____

Judgment Day

Kneeling here before You
Head bowed down
In reverence to my Almighty King

My life flashes by
On this final
Judgment Day

My desire for evil
Permeated my entire existence
Spreading inevitable destruction

My will to serve Yours
Provided a warm flicker of Light
Deep in the center of overwhelming darkness

Weighed on the scale
Of goodness versus evil
My fate should be eternal isolation from You

But by trusting in You
Through Your Son's ultimate sacrifice
I am completely redeemed

Freely passing
Into Your glorious Kingdom
Rejoicing and singing everlasting praise to You

John 5:24-27 "Most assuredly, I say to you, he who hears My word and believes in Him who sent Me has everlasting life, and shall not come into judgment, but has passed from death into life. Most assuredly, I say to you, the hour is coming, and now is, when the dead will hear the voice of the Son of God; and those who hear will live. For as the Father has life in Himself, so He has granted the Son to have life in Himself, and has given Him authority to execute judgment also, because He is the Son of Man.

My Reflections

About the Author

Tom Janicik has been a safety and health professional for the past 25 years. His life's passion is to continue to grow closer to God and to share this experience with others through his writing. In addition, he has collaborated with musicians to develop songs which honor God. He lives in Chesterfield, Missouri, with his daughter Elena and son Tommy who created the inspirational illustrations in the book.

Please send any feedback including life changing stories to yourgiftofgrace@earthlink.net.

CPSIA information can be obtained at www.ICGtesting.com
Printed in the USA
LVOW090737170513

334192LV00001B/1/P